GOING DEEPER IN GOD

Steve Battles

ABOUT THE AUTHOR

Stephen Battles is the founding pastor of Restoration Gospel Lighthouse in Wood River, Illinois - one of several churches he has pastored during 66 years of ministry. He is the president and founder of Restoration Ministries, based in Marine, Illinois.

Steve was called to preach as a young 23 year old seeking and wrestling to know the will of God. He is still going strong at 86. He spent his first 7 years of ministry in Baptist churches. After receiving the baptism in the Holy Spirit, he launched out in faith to minister wherever God opened doors. In addition to pastoral ministry, he has served as a missionary evangelist throughout the USA and

internationally in many nations.

Steve is known as a man of prayer and the

Word. His heart burns with passion to see the

power of God restored to the church, and to

help sincere believers go to a deeper place in

God.

Stephen Battles

TO ORDER MATERIALS OR SCHEDULE MEETINGS

Restoration Ministries

524 Humboldt St., Marine, IL 62061

(618) 541-8986

preacherman7134@yahoo.com

CONTENTS

FOREWORD

Stephen Battles will help you find a

deeper place in God. This book is filled with

wisdom and inspiration from 66 years of

prayer, study and worldwide ministry. Steve

surrendered to the call to preach at the age of

23, after much prayer and contemplation. He is

still going strong at 86.

We have been friends for more than 40 years

and have ministered together on many

occasions in the USA and abroad. His

preaching has always inspired me to rise up in

faith and draw closer to God. Through the

years, Steve has served as a pastor and

missionary evangelist. He is known as a man

of prayer and the Word who passionately pours his heart out in ministry whether he is preaching to 5 or 500.

He often moves in a strong prophetic anointing. God has used him to give me encouraging - and life changing - words at key moments of my life and ministry. I pray that "Going Deeper in God" will impact and inspire you, and strengthen you in your walk with God. It will not only take you to a deeper place in God; it will carry you to higher ground in the Spirit.

Finally, I view my dear friend and brother as a humble spiritual warrior. Steve has fought fierce battles on many fronts throughout 66 years of ministry- and, at 86, he is still

preaching in passion and power and praying

with faith and authority. As you pass through

these pages, you will benefit from the victories

won and the insights gained, over the course of

nearly 7 decades of Spirit filled ministry.

I am honored to recommend "Going Deeper in

God" because I know Steve Battles is a man of

God who handles the Word of God with

integrity. The anointed words on the pages that

follow, are poured out from a burning heart that

desires to help you find a deeper place in God.

Ron Sutton

CHAPTER ONE

The King and His Kingdom

John the Revelator wrote in Rev 1:5 and 6 concerning Jesus and us, I quote: "And from Jesus Christ who is the faithful witness, and the first begotten of the dead, and the prince of the kings of the earth. Unto him that loves us, and washed us from our sins in his own blood, and hath made us kings and priests unto God and his father, to him be glory and dominion forever and ever. A-men!"

The reality of God bringing a people of all

nations together to be kings and priests unto

God is now in our generation, and all the way

back to Calvary, a truth confirmed by the

scriptures and in the hearts of every believer

who has come to God, with a repentance and

faith in the saving power of Jesus Christ. Truly

God has translated us from this world and its

darkness unto the kingdom of his dear Son

(Col. 1:13). He has made us a royal priesthood

and we are now his chosen people (I Peter

2:9-10).

The Church is the Bride of Christ that is being

washed clean by the blood and the word of

God (Ephesians 5:25,26). As His bride, we are

destined to reign with him forever (Rev 9:9,10).
The Church must be distinguished by the
headship of Christ.   It is His Body and He is
the life of the Church. "But speaking the truth
in love, may grow up into Him in all things,
which is the head even Christ. From whom the
whole body fitly joined together and compacted
by that which every joint supplieth according to
the effectual working in the measure of every
part, maketh increase of the body unto the
edifying of itself in love" (Ephesians 4:15-16).

Now the Church is not a Kingdom Hall but it is
a living organism of believers knitted together
in love (Col. 2:2). We are not the Kingdom,

though the kingdom is within us. But we will reign in the kingdom with Christ as King.

There is a kingdom theology that says we are going to be the Kingdom on earth, but that is a twisted application of scriptures. It would do away with the proper terms of the meaning of Christ's Church. We must understand that there are two types of people that God addresses throughout the scriptures. He speaks to the nation of Israel that they would someday inherit the land of promise, but to us he says we are looking for a city whose builder and maker is God. "But now they desire a better country, that is, an heavenly: wherefore

God is not ashamed to be called their God: for he hath prepared for them a city" (Hebrews 11:16).

In the four gospels we find the Lord addressed as a King in Matthew, in Mark as a servant, in Luke as a physician and healer, and in John as the Son of God. The Matthew account speaks of the mysteries of the kingdom (especially Matthew 13). Then the coming in of the kingdom is seen in Matthew 24. This includes Daniel's vision of the kingdom as a stone cut out without hands (Dan 2:43,44). Matthew says "For them shall be great tribulation such as was not since the beginning of the World to this

time, no more ever shall be" (Matthew 24:21).
Kings and kingdoms on earth shall be
destroyed. After this, he will come with all his
saints to set up his millennial reign on
earth. He will establish his kingdom and we
the church will come with him. "Blessed and
holy is he that hath part in the first resurrection;
on such the second death hath no power, but
they shall be priests of God and of Christ, and
shall reign with him a thousand years."

We shall reign over the kingdoms of this world
by being redeemed from the earth by his shed
blood. We have been given authority to rule
now over evil spirits, the flesh and the power of

sin in the world. But then we shall rule over and

judge the kingdoms of the earth. "Do you not

know that the saints shall judge the

world? And if the world shall be judged by you,

are ye unworthy to judge the smallest

matters? Know ye not that we shall judge

angels? How much more things that pertain to

this life" (I Corinthians 6:2,3)?

The kingdom people look for a king and he

shall come as a king to them. When Pilate was

interrogating Jesus He asked, "Are you the

King of the Jews?" He later asked: "Are you a

king" (John 18:33,37). He answered that he

was a king with a kingdom, but it was not of

this world. Then he said "Thou sayest that I

am a king, to this ever was I born and for this

cause came I unto the world that I should bear

witness unto the truth. Everyone that is of the

truth heareth my voice." He is the King of the

Jews but they refused to have him reign over

them. He came to his own , and his own

received him not. He said another would come

in his own name and they would receive

him. The anti-Christ will come as a mighty

leader and they will receive him for a

season. But after a brief time, he will destroy

the peace and great tribulation will occur. At

the end of tribulation, Jesus will come and all

will see him. "Behold, he cometh with clouds

and every eye shall see him and they also

which pierced him; and all kindreds of the earth

shall wail because of him. Even so, Amen"

(Rev 1.7) Notice that they will not rejoice but

wail because they had rejected him. Also

in Zech 12:9-10: "And it shall come to pass in

that day, that I will seek to destroy all the

nations that come against Jerusalem, and I will

pour upon the house of David, and upon the

inhabitants of Jerusalem the spirit of grace and

of supplications: and they shall look upon

me whom they have pierced and they shall

mourn for him as one mourneth for his only

son, and shall be in bitterness for him as one

that is in bitterness for his first born."

There will be no joy in this time for them because they will realize that they failed to recognize him as the true one. In their sorrow they will know they crucified the Lord of glory - their very messiah and real king. The lineage of David, Jesus, was rejected, but he shall be restored as their king. For a thousand years we, the church, shall reign with him over the nations along with the true Israel of God.

When he comes for the church, it is a glorious time of rejoicing. It is our blessed hope. Not sorrow nor tribulation, nor mourning, but praising: "And they sang a new song, saying, thou art worthy to take the book, and to open the seals thereof; for thou wast slain and hast redeemed us to God by thy blood out of every kindred and tongue and people and nation" (Rev 5;9). This is the song of the redeemed. Those that look for him with anticipation will rejoice in that day, for Hs is our Lord and redeemer. "For God hath not appointed us to wrath, but to obtain salvation by our Lord Jesus Christ, who died for us, that whether we wake or sleep, we should live together with him" (I Thessalonians 5:9-10). In every promise to the church concerning the end times it always concludes we are with him - not separated but together with our head and our redeemer.

We have been redeemed to be with him. The government is upon his shoulders Isaiah 9:6 says: "For unto us a child is born, unto us a son is given: and the government shall be upon his shoulder, and he shall be called wonderful counselor, the mighty God, the everlasting Father, the Prince of Peace." In this place of his kingdoms he said, "They shall not hurt nor destroy in all my holy mountain, for the earth shall be full of knowledge of the Lord, as the waters cover the sea; and in that day there shall be a root of Jesse, which shall stand for an ensign of the people to it shall the Gentiles seek: and his rest shall be glorious" (Isaiah 11:9-10).

The Church is his resting-place. He is ours. We shall see his kingdom come and his will be done in earth even as it is in heaven. We are going to come with him to destroy the rulers and wicked and then there will be peace on earth, good will toward all men. Until then we are to be faithful to preach and teach his word, and to turn many to righteousness. "And they that be wise shall sine as the brightness of the firmament: and they that turn many to righteousness as the stars forever and ever" (Daniel 12:3).

The destruction of the earth by fire will prepare

it for the coming of Christ to set up his eternal

kingdom. He is not going to set his kingdom

up until the earth is prepared for such a time. It

will shake like a drunkard and experience all

the terrible things that will occur when the

church is taken out. But when we return, it will

be ready for his majesty to reign and rule. The

earth is utterly broken down, the earth is clean

dissolved, the earth is moved

exceedingly. The earth shall reel to and for like

a drunkard and shall be be removed like a

cottage: and the transgression thereof shall be

heavy upon it: and it shall fall and not rise

again" (Isaiah 24:19,20).

He shall judge the earth but after the purging

there shall be great rejoicing. "Then the moon

shall be confounded, and the sun ashamed,

when the Lord of hosts shall reign in Mount

Zion, and in Jerusalem and before his ancients

gloriously" (Isaiah 24:23). "And He was clothed

with vesture dipped in blood: and his name is

called The Word of God. And the armies which

were in heaven followed him upon white

horses clothed in find linen, white and clean

and out of his mouth goeth a sharp sword that

with it he should smite the nations. And he

shall rule them with a rod of iron, and h

e treadeth the winepress of the fierceness and

wrath of almighty God. And he hath on his

vesture and on his thigh a name written, King

of Kings and Lord of Lords" (Rev 19:13-

16). Everything of rebellion, sin, witchcraft is

cast into the lake of fire - removed off the earth

as he sets up his Kingdom.

What a day that will be when our Jesus we

shall see! He is coming as a conquering king

and we shall follow him. Stay ready for his

appearing. "So Christ was once offered to

bear the sins of many and unto them that look

for him shall he appear the second time without

sin unto salvation" (Hebrews 9:28).

It is not a kingdom now theology that has been

spoken by the Jehovah witnesses, and even by

deceived people in the Church. It is a King

coming with his kingdom. When he comes,

then we shall be kings and priests with him.

We are not here to establish it but to preach a

gospel of a coming Christ, and the glorious

truth that we are separated for him. He is the

center of the whole message - not as a man

of the flesh - but as a resurrected Christ who

will bring a bring a kingdom of

resurrection. Hallelujah!

CHAPTER TWO

"What Pleases God?"

This question is one to take seriously. It could be answered in so many ways. Many books have been written with about countless answers. Some answer it by speaking about the holy life that God desires for us to live. The command of Scripture is: ***"Be ye holy; for I am holy" (I Peter 1:16).*** He wants us to be filled with His righteousness.

(The great theme of the Bible is His desire to have a people for Himself; but what really pleases God, or what is it that God can be satisfied with?)

Let us look at the scripture in Isaiah 53:10,

11. Just quoting from the first part of both

verses, *"Yet it pleased the Lord to*

bruise him;" *"He shall see the travail of his*

soul, and shall be satisfied". The offering of the

Son of God in His crucifixion, as horrible as the

cross was, brought pleasure and satisfaction to

the Father's heart. We wonder in amazement

at the love of God for humanity that He could

allow such a sacrifice for a world of sinners.

That one great act of sacrifice made it possible

for repentant sinners in all generation to be

saved. His love for lost sinners moved him to

say that he was pleased with Jesus suffering and dying on the cross.

In Hebrews 10:6 it says, *"In burnt offerings and sacrifices for sin thou hast had no pleasure."* When God looked on the animal sacrifices of the Old Testament it did not satisfy Him. He was not pleased with the blood and death of animals that were slain for the sins of the people.

It would seem to us that it would have been much easier for God to have received those sacrifices and spared His own son, but this was not enough to please God, not enough to satisfy the justice demanded by holiness. *"He that spared not his own Son, but delivered him up for us all"(Rom 8:32a).* This is the marvel of the grace and mercy of God. Then Jesus said *"Then said I, Lo, I come (in the volume of the book it is written of me,) to do thy will, O God" (Heb. 10:7).* In the Godhead there was no debate as to what it would be that would please God for our redemption. No one could please God, but God Himself.

The whole gospel is what God did, not what anyone else did or ever will do. When we look at the question, "What pleases God?" we can only come up with one real answer, and that is God is only pleased with God. *"Thou art worthy, O Lord, to receive glory and honour,*

and power: for thou hast created all things, and

for thy pleasure they are and were

created"(Rev 4:11). All creation was made for

Him and by Him, but in all that He must be

declared as the only source to be looked upon

that can satisfy Himself.

We can see so much of our own efforts in

church work today trying to please God, and

yet it is only wood, hay and stubble if it is not

Him working in us. You can burn up all kinds

of energy and completely exhaust all your

human efforts, but that will not please

God. We can build churches, make nice

buildings, sweat and labor, and offer up the works of our hands, but to no satisfaction to God. If it is not Him working in us and through us, it will not please God.

Many are quitting the ministry and falling away from the love of God because the work did not originate from the cross and enter into the power of the resurrection. *"For it is God which worketh in you both to will and to do of his good pleasure."* It is His good pleasure and to His satisfaction that He wants to be your willingness, as well as your performance, to carry out His will. We cannot, and never have been able to, please God ourselves. It takes

34

Christ in you to do that, and without Him, all the effort of self is vain and of no value in the economy of eternity.

Without this perspective in our lives we only seek our own. *"For all seek their own, not the thingswhich are Jesus Christ's"(Phil 2:21).*

It is no wonder so many become discouraged and want to quit. When we try with self-effort to please God, then we labor in vain. The fire of God will try each man's work to see what sort it is; it will burn if what we do is in our own energy and strength. Consider I Corinthians 3:10-13. The last part of verse 13 says, *"and the fire shall try every man's work of what sort it is."* Even the evangelizing and methods of ministry to win the lost will go through the fire of God's test. If it is not in and through Christ it will burn, because anything less than the pleasing of God by God through Christ in us is not enough to please the Father.

Only what is done through Christ will last, because that is the only labor that will please the Father. *"Therefore, my beloved brethren, be ye steadfast, unmoveable, always abounding in the work of the Lord, forasmuch as ye know that your labour is not in vain in the Lord"* (I Cor 15:58).

From the pleasing work of Christ at the cross,

He crucified you and I. Out of that death we received the life of Jesus Christ, and this life is what must be our life to please the Father. *"Having made known unto us the mystery of his will, according to his good pleasure which he hath purposed in himself"* *(Eph. 1:9).*

The pleasure of His purpose has to be in us to make Him pleased. So again I say, God can only be pleased by God Himself. When this is fully realized we will give up on trying to please God with our own ability. Christians and leaders often try to take on things that do not need to be taken on. It is mostly done in the name of the Lord, but not in His strength. But

doing it as a work of the flesh will leave God

not pleased nor satisfied.

Again we look at *Eph 1:5-6: "Having*

predestinated us unto the adoption of children

by Jesus Christ to himself, according to the

good pleasure of his will. To the praise of the

glory of his grace, where in he hath made

us accepted in the beloved."

When we try to become accepted and to

perform something that would make us

pleasing to the Father, we negate the whole

redemption sacrifice, and make God to be a

liar. Our self-effort implies that the sacrifice of

His Son was not enough. But it is clear that He

said that He was enough, and that He was

totally pleased with His death and shedding of

blood. This is also called frustrating the grace

of God. *"I do not frustrate the grace of God: for*

if righteousness come by the law then Christ is

dead in vain" (Gal 2:21).

God has only one means of salvation and that

is in Himself, through Jesus Christ shedding

His blood to redeem us. People talk of losing

their salvation. Some will lose it because they

never had His salvation in the first place. It

was not the salvation that was in Christ; it was

one of religion, or emotion but without the

reality of Christ in it. It did not, could not, and

will not please God. He never started

something He did not finish. We are complete

in Him; it has been finished.

"For by grace ye saved through faith; and that

not of yourselves: it is the gift of God" (Eph

2:8). Is it any wonder the Apostle Paul

said, *"But what things were gain to me, those I*

counted loss for Christ" (Phil 3:7). When

we have gained something that results in us

glorying in our flesh, something that gives us a

reputation among men, it robs God of His

rightful place.

All that we gain by flesh will become loss; it will

not make it into eternity. There are so many

encouraging scriptures that tell us to let Christ

work in us. It is from this position we are able

glorify God. Another one is found in *Phil 1:11:*

"Being filled with the fruits ofrighteousness,

which are by Jesus Christ, unto the glory and

praise of God." Notice the fruit is to the praise

of God. It is such a revelation of God's

provision for us to His glory that it causes His

people to praise Him for it all.

No matter which way you approach the subject

of pleasing God, you still come with the same

answer: He, the holy God, could only please

Himself by Himself, and yet remain a God of

humility and mercy to all of us. I am greatly

encouraged by *Phil 1:6: "Being confident of this*

very thing, that he which hath began a good

work in you will perform it until the day of Jesus

Christ."

This work of God was so complete in every

way that He was called the Alpha and

Omega. Nothing started without Him and

nothing ends without Him. He is the opening

and the closing of ages upon ages. He will

soon come in His greater glory to receive those

who are in Christ.

"And when all things shall be subdued unto him

then shall the son also himself be subject unto

him that put all things under him, that God may

be all in all" (I Cor 15:28).

Do you see that all that pleases Him will be

brought to Him in total subjection to His

glory and praise? Hallelujah, people of

God! Rest from your labor and enter into His

rest (Hebrews 4:9,10). One last part of this

message on pleasing God is found in *Heb*

11:6: "But without faith it is impossible to

please him; for he that cometh to God must

believe that he is, and that he is arewarder of

them that diligently seek him."

It takes His faith to be pleasing faith, and that faith comes by hearing the Word of God. We receive into our lives the measure of faith needed, and then give it back to the Lord in prayer and service. He includes us in every way, as we become willing to yield to Him. He is our willingness working His will in our lives.

"Make you perfect in every good work to do his will, working in you that which is well pleasing in his sight, through Jesus Christ, to whom be glory for ever and ever. Amen (Heb 13:21).

I believe we have missed the mark so many times by trying to please God from our own

reasoning and acting on presumption. We
have over extended ourselves with building
projects, and even ministries at times, without it
being His direction. We then presume God is
responsible to support these things. Then,
when He doesn't, they fall flat, fail, and blame
the Lord for not granting their request to
support the work.

I want to reemphasize that God will only
support what originates with Him; nothing else
will stand the rest of time. The faith that comes
from God is accepted and honored by the
Father. Nothing of lasting value ever comes of
anything else. Let us be still to hear and obey

in order to let the Lord guide us into His full

plan. That is what will bring pleasure to Him -

our patience, faith and obedience. Pray this:

"Lord, help me to remain in Your presence to

receive from You the nature of Your Son

Jesus, and to obey Your voice within. Amen."

CHAPTER THREE

Will Your House Stand?

"Whosoever cometh to me, and heareth my sayings, and doeth them, I will show you to whom he is like; He is like a man which built an house, and dug deep and laid the foundation on a rock; and when the flood arose, the stream beat vehemently upon that house, and could not shake it: for it was founded on the rock" (Luke 5:47-48). This passage is an awesome portrayal of soundness. It seems to be a simple revelation of how to become immovable.

Reports and testimonies of Christians today are that they are being tested and tried as never before. Marriages, children, finances, and a host of other things are being affected by a flood of the enemy's power. It has brought so much tension that we need to realize what God has spoken in His word. It is the only foundation on which to stand in order not to fall.

First, we must realize where the adversity is coming from: "And the serpent cast out of his mouth water as a flood after the woman, that he might cause her to be carried away of the flood" (Revelation 12:15). Satan and his demonic forces have been released against the Body of Christ in great fury. Every tactic of aggressive evil power is set against the church to discourage, divide and destroy its effectiveness. The flood of deception and physical and spiritual wounding has been unleashed.

It is leading up to the show down of the ages. "And it was given unto him to make war with the saints, and to overcome them: and power was given him over all kindred, and tongues, and nations. And all that dwell upon the earth shall worship him, whose names are not written in the book of life of the Lamb slain from the foundation of the world" (Revelation 13: 7-

8). The reality of our need to be solid in

Christ has come upon us. We are engaged in

the preliminary battle of the ages. Our house

will stand if we are rooted and grounded and

settled on the Rock of Jesus Christ and His

teachings. "But Christ as a son over his own

house are we, if we hold fast the confidence

and the rejoicing of the hope firm unto the end"

(Hebrews 3:6).

Luke described a great flood that would beat

vehemently upon the house built on a rock; the

flood could not shake it. We cannot know the

solidness of what we are built on without the

testing and trying of our faith. It is in the

everyday walk that we prove to be who we are

in Christ. We must purge ourselves of any

wrong ways and selfish choices. II Timothy

2:21 says: "If a man therefore will purge

himself from these, he shall be a vessel

unto honour sanctified, and meet for the

master's use, and prepared unto every good

work."

We must live a consistent life in Christ. He is

the great I AM and will establish us in all the

ways of righteousness. Mark 3:27 says: "No

man can enter into a strong man's house, and

spoil his goods, except he first bind the strong

man; and then he will spoil his house." Jesus was teaching here about a house divided that cannot stand.

I would like to apply this to our personal lives. If we are strong in the Lord, we can guard our house and the enemy cannot spoil us. When we give into temptation and allow a door to be opened to the world, flesh and the devil, we are going to fall. It is as sure as the sunrise of a new day.

The only guarantee of our not being overcome are the promises of God that we obtain and hold by faith. "For if these things be in you, and abound, they make you that ye shall neither be barren nor unfruitful in the knowledge of our

Lord Jesus Christ. But he who lacketh these

things is blind and cannot see afar off, and

hath forgotten that he was purged from his

old sins. Wherefore the rather, brethren, give

diligence to make your calling and election

sure: for if you do these things, ye shall never

fall" (2 Peter 1:8-10.)

It is the collapse of our homes, our marriages,

our personal victory that will occur when we do

not give heed to what the Lord has called us

into. Neglect of these things results in

ministries and churches falling from the

testimony of holiness and the presence of God

among them.

We have committed a terrible atrocity in trying to make the gospel "user friendly." We have created a gospel and established churches that are no longer scriptural. We want something so badly, we sell out for success. In so doing, we give ground to evil spirits through compromise.

The house will not stand that is built on earthly principles - principles like positive thinking rooted in psychology and mind science. "Now the Spirit speaketh expressly that in the latter times some shall depart from the faith, giving heed to seducing spirits, and doctrines of devils" (I Timothy 4-1).

It is happening very rapidly. The love of fame and fortune has taken control until few desire to take a godly stand against the evil flood that is coming out of the enemy's mouth. "And if it seem evil unto you to serve the Lord, choose you this day whom ye will serve; whether the gods which your fathers served that were on the other side of the flood, or the gods of the Amorites, in whose land ye dwell, but as for me and my house, we will serve the Lord" (Joshua 24:15). This is a choice we must make.

Which side of the flood do you want to stand

on? The flood in this case was the one God

sent to destroy the wicked on the earth. Joshua

said he was going to serve the God who saved

Noah and his family. He understood that after

the flood, you still have an enemy whose

ground you are on. Your choice, upon this

realization, is crucial: you will either choose the

god of this world or the Lord God who created

all things for His pleasure.

The God of this world has not changed. "But if

our gospel be hid, it is hid to them who are lost:

In whom the god of this world hath blinded the

minds of them which believe not, lest the light

of the glorious gospel of Christ, who is the

image of God, should shine unto them" (2

Corinthians 4:3-4).

Darkness and blindness are what happen

when we serve the wrong God. If we build in

the darkness that comes from disobedience to

the Word, our house will fall when the flood

comes. We have to be anchored in Christ. Our

heart must be His throne. No other must be

allowed to rule over the house, but Him alone.

He is the only Lord God Almighty.

"For We know that if our earthly house of this

tabernacle were dissolved, we have a building

of God, a house not made with hands, eternal

in the heavens. For in this we groan, earnestly

desiring to be clothed upon with our house

which is from heaven" (2 Corinthians 5:1-2).

What is eternal has been forever established;

it can never be shaken. Our problems

arise because we are too attached to the

temporary. Everything that seen will one day

pass away. When the church is built on the

wisdom and ways of man, it will fall with all

other temporary things.

When we come to the fullness of Christ, we

find substance not tangible to the physical, but

lived in by the spiritual man. He will stand

because his house is eternal, and all the floods

of the enemy cannot destroy it. "For all things

are for your sakes, that the abundant grace

might through the thanksgiving of many

redound to the glory of God. For which cause

we faint not; but through our outward man

perish, yet the inward man is renewed day by

day" (2 Corinthians 4:15-16).

CHAPTER FOUR

Winds of Adversity

The seasons of adversity seem to come in times when the church least expects them. We are a people that are vulnerable to the sneak attack, if we do not stay in the walk of the Spirit filled life. There are several ways the enemy can come with the winds of adversity and bring defeat. He is determined to keep us from the victory. He desires to hinder and prevent the truth from being released through us. Victory is our lot when we remain in unbroken fellowship with the Lord

Jesus Christ. He alone is a secure refuge and fortress. In Him, we can face adversity and overcome adversaries.

One of the winds mentioned in the scriptures is the wind of doctrine. The Apostle Paul wrote to the church in Ephesus: "that we henceforth be no more children tossed to and fro and carried about with every wind of doctrine, by the sleight of men and cunning craftiness, whereby they lie in wait to deceive" (Ephesians 4:14).

The doctrines of men, and the teaching of those who come with something more attractive, is to always allure you into following deception. It is the enemy's trick to use truth mixed with a lie to lead people astray.

Many make the fatal error of pursuing an

experience instead of the truth of the Word of

God. The Holy Spirit Himself has come to keep

us from being deceived, but we must be

diligent to study the Word of God. It is our

greatest safeguard against deception.

"Howbeit when He, the Spirit of truth, is come

He will guide you into all truth" (John 16:13). It

is clear that God does not want us to be blown

about the shifting winds of false teachers and

deceptive teaching.

With the spread of Christian television, we are

subjected to a flood of different ministries and

teachings. Discernment is greatly needed. We must be aware of false brethren and alert to false doctrines. Paul the Apostle told young Timothy, as he mentored him and helped him to stay with the truth: "For the time will come when they will not endure sound doctrine, but after their own lusts shall they heap to themselves teachers, having itching ears; and they shall turn away their ears from the truth, and shall be turned unto fables" (1 Timothy 4:2).

There is an abundance of teachers that are very clever in what they say; they are and glad to make followers of you and me. We are in a generation of people that continually want

some new thing, some experience, that will

tickle their ears and keep them excited.

It is a sleight of hand to make you think

something is real when it is not. Like a

magician they pull things up out of the

scriptures and have some way to make it look

like the truth. But, in reality, it is a lie out of the

pits of darkness. Some peddle new revelations,

and claim that no one else has seen it like this

before.

This is the method of deceivers and apostates.

The wind of doctrinal error is taking the modern

day church into deception and delusion. It is

causing many to depart from the faith once delivered to the saints. "Now the Spirit speaketh expressly that in the latter times some shall depart from the faith, giving heed to seducing spirits, and doctrines of devils" (I Timothy 4:1).

The solution to all this is very simple, and will keep us in the right way of the light of the Word of God. In the scriptures it is declared in this manner: "Study to show thyself approved unto God, a workman that needeth not to be ashamed, rightly dividing the word of truth" (2 Timothy 2:15).

We can never be sure of the teachers unless

we are willing to search the Scripture and let it speak for itself. "All scripture is given by inspiration of God, and is profitable for doctrine, for reproof, for correction, for instruction in righteousness: that the man of God may be thoroughly furnished unto all good works" (2Timothy 3:16).

Notice that when the doctrine is right we will do what is right. False teaching is designed to get us doing what is not right. False teachers twist the meaning of Scripture and lead us to justify our sins by using the Word of God deceitfully. Misapplying it in such a way causes us to sear our conscience and walk in the error of our own ways.

Then there are the winds of adversity that blow in a way that Job described in Job 30:15-16: "Terrors are turned upon me: they pursue my soul as the wind: and my welfare passeth away as a cloud. And now my soul is poured out upon me; the days of affliction have taken hold upon me."

This would describe a lot of situations that some are going through these days. We are all in a world that is often not pleasant and care free. The trials that befall the child of God can do one of two things. It can drive us closer to the reality that we have a God who is our shelter in the time of storm, and a Rock of refuge from the evil one, or it can cause us to withdraw into the oppression that the enemy wants us to sink down into.

There are times that we must know how to pray as King David did when he said: "Hide not thy face from me in the day when I am in trouble, incline thine ear unto me: in the day when I call answer me speedily. For my days are consumed like smoke, and my bones are burned as a hearth" (Ps.102:2-3). We try to keep our head up and do all the positive things that are possible to overcome, but if the Lord does not deliver it is of no use.

David again said: "Why art thou cast down, O my soul? And why art thou disquieted with in me? Hope thou in God: for I shall yet praise Him, who is the health of my countenance, and my God" (Ps 42:11).

Jesus, the master of all circumstances, gave a promise that many don't want to embrace. He did not give it to make us fear the danger or the trial, but to tell us to expect such things, and to not be ignorant that they would come. He didn't want us to be taken by surprise.

It is foolish to think that the Christian life is always a soft bed of blessings with out testing. Here is what He said to prepare us:

"These things I have spoken unto you, that in Me ye might have peace. In the world ye shall have tribulation: but be of good cheer: I have overcome the world" (John16:33).

It is not always easy to understand what triggers the trial, or the test. But when it comes, we must know what to do - trust the Lord and hold on by faith to his word. Our reaction to the situation will make the difference between victory and defeat. It is like the tornado when it comes. If you know how to go through the storm, you come out okay. But if you do not, then it is destructive to all you have.

We must believe that what the devil brings to

destroy us, God can use to develop us. Peter

said, "Beloved think it not strange concerning

the fiery trial which is to try you, as though

some strange thing happened unto you. But

rejoice, inasmuch as ye are partakers of

Christs sufferings; that when His glory shall be

revealed ye may be glad also with exceeding

joy" (1 Pet. 4:12-13).

It is important that we respond with praise to

the Lord. This is is not easy when the wind is

blowing and the adversary is saying, "you are

forgotten, and you will not make it through this

one." That is when we have to shake off the

heavy bands and lift up holy hands and give

thanks to the Lord. That is when we must cast

ourselves upon Him alone.

I have written and preached a lot of messages

on suffering, and the end results. It doesn't get

easier than it was at the beginning of our walk

with the Lord. It all comes down to this: we

have to cast our care on Him and He will do

the rest. The Lord enables us to walk in

total victory - victory which He has provided in

Christ. That is truly the only victory we can

depend upon.

You can say, "None of this applies to me," but

as you continue on to know the Lord in deeper

ways, the winds of adversity will blow. The

enemy sends them to keep you from making

progress. You must meet them in faith and

refuse to be driven back by opposition and

resistance. In the face of adversity, we must

pursue the presence of the Lord daily.

Much of what happens to us is to prepare us to

help others to be set free. Paul related to this

when he wrote to Corinth and said, "Blessed

be God, even the Father of our Lord Jesus

Christ, the Father of mercies, and the God of

all comfort. Who comforteth us in all our

tribulation, that we may be able to comfort

them which are in any trouble, by the comfort

wherewith we ourselves are comforted of God"

(2 Cor. 1:4).

What the adversity is all about is to bring us into the image of the Son of God. His image must be seen in us. It has to be obvious to others. And it will be as we are developed through good times and adverse times. Coming through problems and trials victoriously will prepare us to minister deliverance and healing to the broken hearted.

It is needful for each one in the Body of Christ to walk in uprightly and victoriously in the Lord, not just for ourselves but for others. of our Lord When we believe that we are truly conquers through the power of the name of Jesus, we

can help lead others from defeat to victory.

Our Savior is the triumphant Christ. In Him,

there is nothing impossible to them that

believe. He will never fail those who put their

trust in Him. It makes no difference how the

winds blow against the child of God; we can

emerge with victory from the storm. When

storms are met in faith, we go deeper into the

abiding life in Christ.

Jesus is our Rock, our fortress, and our

deliverer. Nothing can defeat the One who has

won all the battles; and He has given us the

victory. Through the atonement and the power

of His blood, we rise in faith to defeat the enemy. We have been given faith to know that the deliverer is greater than any circumstance or condition no matter how hard the wind blows. He is the stability of our times, "And wisdom and knowledge shall be the stability of the times, and strength of salvation, the fear of the Lord is his treasure" (Isa.33:6).

This is a not an easy road. Christianity is at war with the powers of darkness. As we walk with the Lord, we will need supernatural strength. "If thou faint in the day of adversity, thy strength is small" (Prov.24:10). We must be those who wait upon the Lord to renew our strength

(Isaiah 40).

The one who is our strength is mighty. He will never fail. It is a time to be strong in the Lord and in the power of His might (Eph 6:10). He will sustain the ones who put their trust in Him. So be encouraged to stand and not give up to the adversary. The winds of adversity will blow, but know that He is the Master of the wind.

When the disciples were in a storm at sea, they woke Him with words that astounded Him. They said, "Lord we perish, and He said why do you have such fear, o ye of little faith, and he rebuked the winds and the sea; and there was a great calm" (Matt 8:26). When He stands

up in our lives,   the winds cease and the storm

comes to nothing. Praise the name of Jesus.

He will only allow enough to happen to bring

you to a new realm of faith in God. He is the

Lord of all and knows how much is needed to

bring you to total surrender.

It is good to have resistance because without

it, we know not the power of the Lord we serve.

It makes us know our need of His life working

in us the nature of His will.

Now may the Lord and the grace of God

in Christ Jesus keep you stable to do His will,

and sanctify you in your spirit, soul and

body. "Therefore; my brethren dearly beloved and longed for, my joy and crown, so stand fast in the Lord, my dearly beloved" (Phil.4:1). "You are the beloved and He has made you to be accepted in the beloved Lord Jesus Christ" (Eph 1:6). God bless and keep you in the position of the conquering one who has saved you for this time and season. Amen